POLAR BEARS

BY GAIL GIBBONS

HOLIDAY HOUSE · NEW YORK

Special thanks to James Doherty,
General Curator at the New York
Zoological Society, Bronx, New York

Library of Congress Cataloging-in-Publication Data
Gibbons, Gail.
Polar bears / by Gail Gibbons.
p.   cm.
ISBN 0-8234-1593-7 (hardcover)
ISBN 0-8234-1768-9 (paperback)
1. Polar bear—Juvenile literature.
[1. Polar bear. 2. Bears] I. Title.
QL737.C27 G48 2001
599.786—dc21
00-054075

To Scott Jacob,
a great postmaster

POLAR BEAR

The snow blows, the wind howls. The temperature is very cold, hovering around −30 degrees Fahrenheit (−34 degrees Celsius). Through the snowy scene a great white bear appears, the polar bear.

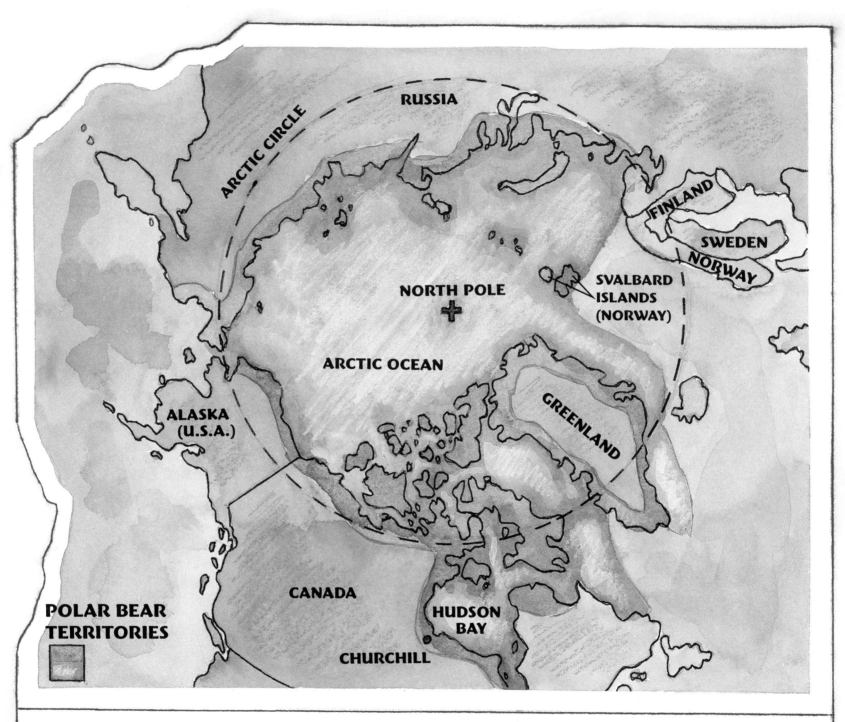

The polar bear lives in the Arctic, the area that surrounds the North Pole. Part of the Arctic is frozen, treeless land called tundra. Most of the Arctic is ocean. Ice covers the water most of the year.

Only a few animals such as seals, Arctic foxes, walruses and Arctic terns can survive in such a cold and hostile climate. The polar bear is the biggest and most powerful of them all.

MALE

Scientists call
the polar bear
URSUS MARITIMUS,
meaning "sea bear."

Bears belong to the family called Ursidae. Of the eight bears in
this family, the polar bear is the largest. Most scientists believe
polar bears have been living on earth about 100,000 years.

FEMALE

An average male polar bear is so big that when it stands on its hind legs it may be as tall as 10 feet (3 meters). It usually weighs 750 pounds (340 kilograms) to 1100 pounds (500 kilograms). A female polar bear is about two-thirds that size.

POLAR BEAR CHARACTERISTICS

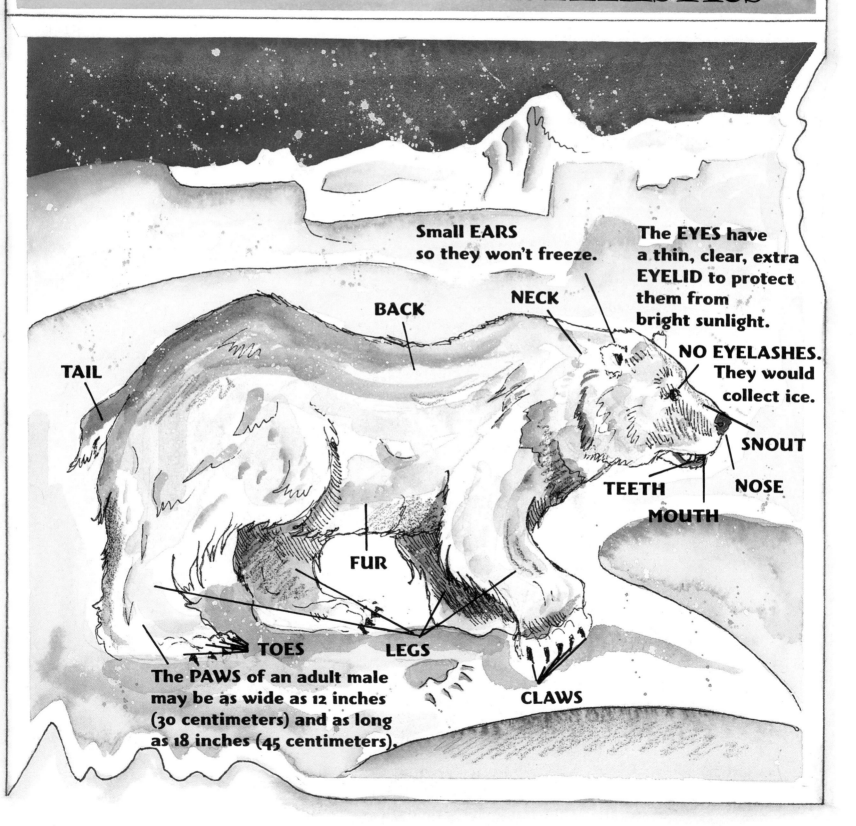

Small EARS so they won't freeze.

The EYES have a thin, clear, extra EYELID to protect them from bright sunlight.

NO EYELASHES. They would collect ice.

BACK

NECK

TAIL

SNOUT

TEETH

NOSE

MOUTH

FUR

TOES

LEGS

CLAWS

The PAWS of an adult male may be as wide as 12 inches (30 centimeters) and as long as 18 inches (45 centimeters).

The bottom of a polar bear's paw has rough pads and fur to keep it from slipping on ice. The fur also helps keep the paw warm.

WEBBING

PADS

FUR

Polar bears are huge but they are fast, graceful and athletic. They can run 30 miles (50 kilometers) an hour for short distances. They can swim for at least 40 miles (65 kilometers). Polar bears have partially webbed paws for swimming.

Polar bears have an amazing sense of smell. Some scientists believe they can smell a seal more than 3 miles (5 kilometers) away. They can see well in both the light and the dark, and can hear well, too.

Grrrr . . . Polar bears have ways to communicate. When angry or upset these solitary animals growl, hiss, show their teeth and lower their heads and ears.

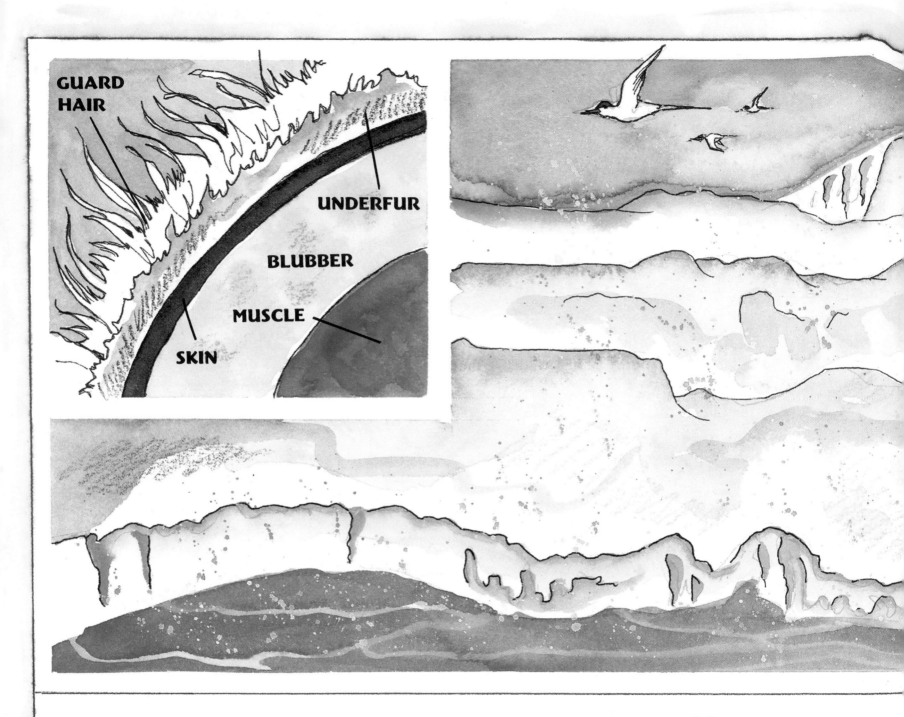

GUARD HAIR

UNDERFUR

BLUBBER

MUSCLE

SKIN

A polar bear's top layer of fur is made up of hollow guard hairs that are colorless but look white. These guard hairs are waterproof and trap air to help keep the bear dry and warm. Below the guard hair and next to the skin is dense underfur.

Under the fur is black skin that takes in heat from sunlight. The polar bear's fur keeps the heat next to the bear's body. Under the skin is a layer of fat called blubber. It is almost 3 inches (7.5 centimeters) thick and helps to insulate the polar bear's body from the cold.

Polar bears are carnivores. That means they eat meat. They are patient hunters. Their favorite food is the ringed seal.

Often a polar bear looks for a breathing hole in the ice where a seal can come up to get air. The bear waits, sometimes for hours. When a seal pops up, the bear swats it with its powerful paw, then pulls the seal from the water with its teeth.

Sometimes a polar bear creeps slowly toward a seal. When the bear gets close, it pounces on the seal. Other times the bear quietly floats in the frigid water. It looks like a chunk of sea ice slowly drifting toward the seal. When the bear is close enough, it grabs the seal.

Scavengers wait to clean up the rest of the kill.

ARCTIC FOX

IVORY GULL

ARCTIC TERN

During the winter, male polar bears, and females that aren't going to have babies called cubs, spend most of their time hunting. A polar bear is able to catch a seal about every five days. Most of the time the bear only eats the seal's skin and blubber. It can eat as much as 150 pounds (68 kilograms) of blubber at one time. They also eat walruses, small whales, fish and other sea life, too.

During the late spring and summer, the ice breaks up. Seals are hard to find. Polar bears hunt and eat musk oxen, caribous and seabirds. When they can't be found, the bears eat berries, mushrooms and seaweed. When late fall and winter return they will hunt seals once again.

During the spring, female and male polar bears come together to mate. After several days they leave each other. During the summer, they continue to hunt for food.

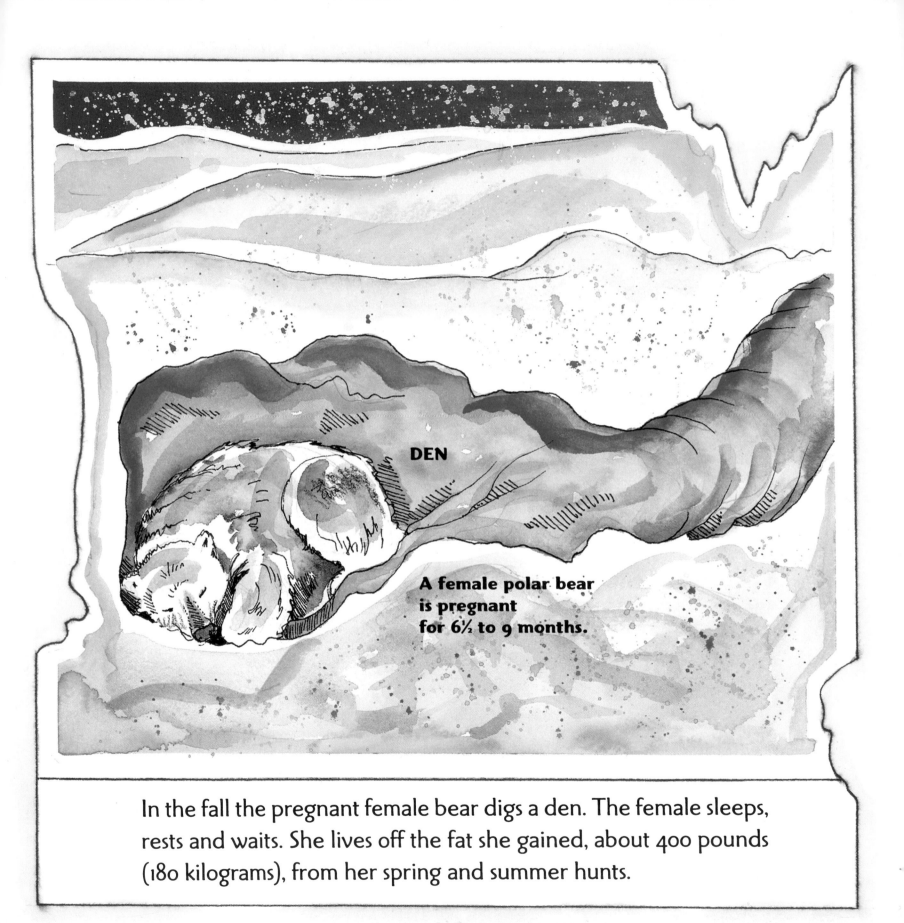

DEN

A female polar bear
is pregnant
for 6½ to 9 months.

In the fall the pregnant female bear digs a den. The female sleeps, rests and waits. She lives off the fat she gained, about 400 pounds (180 kilograms), from her spring and summer hunts.

Cubs nestle in their mother's fur.

In the winter the cubs are born. The mother may have one to four cubs. At birth their eyes are closed; they can't hear; they have only a thin coat of fur; and they weigh a little over one pound (450 grams).

The cubs suckle their mother's rich milk. They snuggle deep in their mother's fur and sleep. Outside the den the winds howl and the temperature is very cold.

By the time the cubs are three weeks old they can hear. About one week later their eyes open. During the first month the cubs grow to be four times larger than their birth size.

Now the cubs are two months old. They can walk and romp around the den. The cubs play together and with their mother, too. Their bodies are furry.

When the cubs are about three months old they leave the den, but stay close to it for the first week. They want to get used to their new outside world. Now the cubs look like small fluffy dogs.

Soon the mother takes the cubs out on the ice to learn about hunting. They watch her get food. She will protect them from any danger.

When it's too cold to hunt, any polar bear may dig a den for protection.

The cubs stay with their mother for about two years until they are almost full grown. During that time, they learn how and where to hunt, how to protect themselves and how to dig dens. Then they go off on their own. Eventually the females will raise their own cubs.

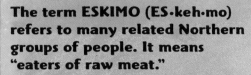

The term ESKIMO (ES·keh·mo) refers to many related Northern groups of people. It means "eaters of raw meat."

INUIT (IN·u·wat) is the term Eskimos in most of Canada use to identify themselves. It means "the people."

INUPIAT (en·NEW·piat) is the term for Eskimo people of Northern Alaska and is the term they prefer. It means "the real people."

Polar bears are big and powerful. People are their main enemy. For thousands of years people living in the Arctic hunted polar bears for their meat and fur. Later, people came from far away places to hunt polar bears for sport. Many bears were killed.

Around 1970, there was concern about the polar bear's ability to survive. There were only about 5,000 left. Laws were passed to stop nearly all the hunting. Because of their beliefs and heritage some native peoples are still allowed a limited hunt. Today, scientists believe there are 20,000 to 40,000 polar bears in the wild.

GLOBAL WARMING is the gradual increase in the temperature of the earth's atmosphere.

Other dangers still exists for polar bears. Drilling for oil and gas can cause pollution. Dangerous chemicals travel by wind to the Arctic from industrial areas. If global warming continues, many scientists and other people are concerned there will be less Arctic ice and therefore less area for the bears to hunt.

Today, scientists keep track of the great white bears. People want to know more about them. Some are seen at zoos. Others live in protected areas. If enough people care, polar bears will be around for a long time.

POLAR BEAR PAW PRINTS

Polar bears have the same body temperatures as humans, 98.6 degrees Fahrenheit (37 degrees Celsius).

The temperature in the Arctic can get as low as –58 degrees Fahrenheit (–50 degrees Celsius).

Scientists have seen polar bears swim more than 40 miles (65 kilometers). They can swim four miles (6.5 kilometers) per hour.

Native peoples of the North call the polar bear Nanook. Traditionally, they respect the strength and power of polar bears and believe they have souls. After killing a polar bear, they thank the bear's soul.

Native people tell many stories and legends about polar bears and make beautiful carvings of them.

All polar bears live in Alaska, Canada, Greenland, Norway and Russia.

Polar bears and penguins never meet because penguins live in the southern hemisphere and polar bears live in the northern hemisphere.

To find food some polar bears have to migrate. Others don't need to.

In the fall, many tourists travel to the town of Churchill in Manitoba, Canada, to watch polar bears. The bears come to wait for the ice to form on Hudson Bay, so they can start hunting there.

The world's largest national park, The Northeast Greenland National Park, was established in 1973 where polar bears are protected.

Polar bears in the wild may live to be 30 years old.